SKY

SONGS

album one
somewhere
murmur

the rift
dawn • the veiled men
where do i go again
moon water farm • my favorite blue
til my body breaks again • momentary • kite
such and such and so on • memory of failure • the end is here

album one

somewhere murmur

inspired by

Taylor Swift • phoebe bridgers
Katherine Li • Gracie Abrams
CHVRCHES • Charlotte Lawrence

the rift

there was a horse
on the unpaved road
and a man and a carriage
full of watermelons

he called for us all of us—
wheels clacking as he rode
his horse drawn carriage
calling for us

there was a boy
on a red brick wall
his feet dangling high in the air
above the sidewalk

he watched this strange world—
slapping his knees
with his small hands
and asked the man to stay

more than four decades later
the boy was now a man or
that thing closer to death
asking the boy to stay

on the wall
dangling feet
calling for him

to jump
to jump into his arms
to jump into his future
to jump into the confusion to come

calling for him

to jump
to jump into terror
to jump into his life

calling for me
calling for me
calling for me

to find my way
back
home

dawn

she said down
and i saw dawn

did i tell you?

i've been hallucinating about hecate
& a castle on fire

did i tell you?

i keep forgetting what dawn is
—sunrise or sunset

coming to the light
coming to the dark

i reached for her hand
as the days dissolved

to speak to your skin folding
—becoming the landscape

on mondays
i hold my face

when my therapist
tells me to ask you
to tell me our secrets
before it's too late

ask your dad, she tells me,
ask him before he is gone

get the secrets, she says,
of the back alley where
we hear you crying

she said dawn
and i saw you

going to the dark
going to the light

i saw your dawn
i heard myself

going to the light
going to the dark

the veiled men

in the kitchen
the men stood screaming

it sounded like laughter
their faces veiled by
cigarette smoke

i lost my mother in the hallway
and when i turned the corner into
the living room
i remembered

she was never there

and the men came and stood
in front of me
half drunk bottles of johnny walker reds
in their hands

they stood screaming
like they were laughing

i stood still waiting for heaven to part
the sea, but only the men noticed

each year i think of them
they grow taller

each day i remember them
their screams sound like laughter

and they said
waving their bottles above their heads

they said
leaning down to be closer
to my wet face

your father
that son of a bitch

your father
where the hell is he

they said

your father
does he think he is closer to god

they said

your father
he is going to die

they were laughing
it sounded like laughing

someone pulled me out of the house by my hand
someone pulled me away from them

the men
in the smoke
in my space

and i heard screaming
and i heard laughing

long after
the men were gone

where do i go again

once in time
my father walked so much faster
than the rest of us
the distance between us
stretching with
each step to miles

tonight thinking of
him as i look back
and call with anger
hurry up come to me
to my body

what if i was to lose my bones
what if i was to lose my yellow skin
this broken mess of a home
the only one i've known

what if this distance between
my heart and my open hand
grows stretches from feet to oceans

i thought—over the sky, somewhere
in the shadows between storms i will learn
a kindness and think i too deserve it

where do i go again
where do i go
where do i go again

to put myself together

what if i could close this distance

that i stopped tending to as it grew
to feet to miles to oceans
to panic attacks to breakdowns

and sing to the moon
and hear someone somewhere
murmur

and it sounds like
the peace between
the in and the out
of breathing

moon water farm

where do we go from a tuesday 10:45pm
when the car outside is covered in ice
and your cycle is off

because if i could have my madness now
i'd be able to find the road
back to how

it was back when i was a child
it was back where i was a child

where do we go from now 11:17
on the same tuesday when i hear
my father's voice scolding me to pray
but i've forgotten how to kneel

only if i could have my mania now
then i could write twelve poems
that will save me

like it did back when i was a child
like it did back where i was a child

where do i go from my life
covered in ice on a tuesday
the day fractured like my mind

where did you go, madness
when i need you to take me back

to that time, that time i was child
to that place, that place where i was found on

the moon
the water
the farm

madness
won't you guide me back
to when i was dying in the wild

my favorite blue

my favorite blue
is skin startled to life

this outside of my body
left to fend for too long

my favorite blue
is the path between my hours

that holds me until i lose
everything else

like my father's face
surrounded by blue winter

sky as i looked up
from his hands

but first let me confess
there are two of me:

this one blue bruised
secrets locked tight

a jaw trapped
below the heart

the other
a memory of a boy

who discovered words in
the back of a blue VW

the carrying of multiples
never lasts long enough

everything comes to an end

like that blue of a gun
shot that scatters the sun

like this blue of my body
frozen in transit

between heaven
and sky

til my body breaks again

he never would have wanted a son
to be the kind that writes love songs

to his father, even as he couldn't
keep from crying in an august afternoon

after lunch, at the door of his apartment,
an embrace a little longer than he'd meant

where does that leave us at the end
of his book, the one that somewhere begins

with a clarinet in a mountain
calling to god and ends broken

in a small room
in little tokyo

he never meant for us to live through
a pandemic across the country from each other

through heart attacks (he)
and mental breakdowns (me)

or through a life without grandchildren
or houses surrounded by grass green

momentary

shatter me

until i can reflect   your disappointment

in endless

                                         pieces

leave me

to tremble in the rust of your arms

embracingdeath

what do you see

in the moment

that momentary longing

from your open door as you watch me

                              walk

away

do you count the seconds

                                         and my steps
the breaths

i drop
                    from my hands

too weak to excavate

your love from your bones

some time later when i am sitting on a train i look for
your leg the one rising taller than any tree as i gripped
on to it terrified of losing you to the momentum of a life
i will never get to choose

what do you see
when you long for me

what do you see

momentary

     moment

the tree you were sure
would grow on foreign soil

if you could just pray hard enough
and believe

kite

give me your hand
i will recognize it by its rhymes

a fraction of what it was
when i thought it could hold up
the earth and the moon
and everything and the sun

give me your hand
i still recognize it by its regrets

let your skin
slip away from you
and i will build a roof
and walls around
your bones

give me your hand
i will call it home

and imagine my own family
a daughter pointing at a photo of you
holding me in your right arm

give me your hand
hold it still like the mountain

when we'd go visit grandpa
and i held out my hand
until the dragonfly
landed on my outstretched finger

you showed me

how to tie the string to its tail
and watched it flap its wings

and hover in front of me

a kite, i said
and held the string
and ran around grandpa's grave
as you shook your head
your lips moving to mutter
a secret to god

give me your hand
i want to hold you

like this
in front of me

fly
dad

fly

such and such and so on

they'd always say
robert looked like my father
and his father
and so on and such and such

there is a photo
of him in black and white
smaller than the house plant
he is hiding behind

playing peekaboo with grandpa
the one who looks like father
and my brother
and so on and such and such

there are no none of me
playing with anyone
but there is one i'm with my family
and looking so concerned

i can't remember the terror
out of frame
in front of me

what was i told?
what did i see?

there was always a pause
assessing all the people
i am not

whatever you are told
when you a child lost in an alley

in nations in which you don't belong

you will believe it
because it's survival

learn to smile and nod in languages
that spell out your death

until you stop
and shape words into bricks
and build walls tall enough
and build walls close enough

together to look like nobody
to speak so only you can understand

to spend the time you have left
climbing to heaven on your own

memory of failure

last week when i returned home
to visit you you pushed the plate
of sliced eggs closer to me
and i closed my eyes trying to create

a moment i could put aside my fear
and ask you about the woman
on the steps in our house in korea
if she was really a ghost like you

told me and you waved your hand
in the air between us
while you told me the cancer
is traveling between us

making this space wider
and my words hide in my bones
until i am silent smiling afraid to
lose this thing called home

because where do we go
if i can manage to stop shaking
long enough to look at your face to
ask you if that ghost that i've been chasing

was not a ghost at all
how can i be unscared
to ask if the the woman
on the stairs was my mother

the one whose hand i held
on an impossible third floor
the one with the hole

in her stomach before

she disappeared into nightmares
and what i always believed to be true
a life, a thought, a desire
and if she was my mother

then who are you to me
then who am i to you
then who are you in my life
then who am i if i can just be

unafraid enough to ask
before i forget you too

what am i to you my father
but your memory of failure

what am i to you
but an early morning regret

the end is here

around the table
we talk about my father
over a roast beef lunch

mom nudging his left arm
motioning for him to place
more of the thinly sliced
meat on the electric skillet

we can't stop his body
from disappearing

doctor told me that the cancer
won't matter, dad says, because
my heart will kill me first.

i just realized this sounds
like a country western song

this sounds like a country western
in a wood paneled bar fronting a band

this sounds like a country western
for all of us without a land

family i think
is gibberish words
uttered holy and repeated

from generation to generation
from one to the next
from me to you

and we say

selah
selah

selah
alleluia

selah

selah

selah

selah

amen
amen

selah

album two
ugly

best laid plans
ugly
held
crazy
little tokyo
under my steps
sky song
called the rain
the last one
questions

album two

ugly

inspired by

Tommy Lefroy • Gracie Abrams
Lykke Li • Taylor Swift

best laid plans

each time he left
for america, for new york

his best laid plans
kept in the pile of his secrets

i chased all the strays
into our backyard

and hid myself in the shrubs
by the front windows

to become invisible
and powerful

and when i was covered completely
i'd jump out and scare the dogs

making them scramble
down the driveway into the night

at nights in a room of open windows
and moths clinging to the ceilings

don't open your eyes, mother would say
don't open your eyes or you will go blind

don't open your eyes, mother would say
don't open your eyes until he returns

and i stayed curled up
in the middle of the bed

eyes closed tight
to keep blindness away

        don't open your eyes, mother would say
        don't open your eyes or you will go blind

he kept coming home
he kept going to america

        don't open your eyes, mother would say
        don't open your eyes until he returns

until i ran to keep up
and i ran to catch up

        don't open your eyes, mother would say
        don't open your eyes or you will go blind

all the way to the water
all the way to a dream

        don't open your eyes, mother would say
        don't open your eyes until he returns

all the way to the water
all the way to a dream

to watch
to a wave on the verge
of rising

ugly

there is nothing
like this of me—

a black & white photo
that tells of my origin

in any of the dozen
albums my father

stole from his siblings
when their mother

passed away
the grandma who

didn't hate me
like the other one

but left her scent
on my pillow

during her last
visit to los angeles

as if she wanted
to erase me

i've spent
embarrassingly many hours

asking myself
if i looked like mother

or father and not
knowing which

answer my heart
was needing to find

but questions
when unanswered

take your life
in handfuls like dirt

until you are
just a mound

ugly
and on the verge

of collapsing
into the sea

you erased
like your grandma

wanted when
she last saw you

that last time she had
to see you still here

ugly
and on the verge

of collapsing into the
mess you've made

of your life
waiting

for answers that
you already knew

in your heart
ugly collapsing

not like mother
not like father
not like mother
not like father

not like
anything
really

not like
anything

held

her arms are strangers
even all these years later

fifty four and counting toward
a place to call home safer

than a july trip to a lake
somewhere north of LA

the sun reminds me that
burning is the start of desire

that breaks what›s left of your tired
body confused in places

that refused you a bit of grace
and i wanted more than the boats

crashing waves and fireworks
and false stories told

about how we found
life in wars

what do you call longing
when it's neverending

do i mistake it for failure
or some punishment for

a crime i committed
in a past i'd regret

if i could recollect it
if i could reclaim it

her arms wrapped around
my shaking body is what

i've been waiting all these years
wanting—to be held by her

what it would have meant to be
called son called beloved

where it would have sent me
if i could remember being held

by her while i was breaking

in a room few feet away

in a house a town away

in a flight for my life
a galaxy away

in this body
hollow and heavy

immovable
and weightless

crazy

back in los angeles for a little
while and i'll get to be here for

my father's 86th birthday,
my mother's too, her 83rd.

it gets harder and harder to
say that i am returning home

the pandemic has made me feel
that i only exist between the walls

of our apartment in pittsburgh

dad's cancer returned
and mom fell again on her way

to the kitchen for water to swallow
the pain on her tongue wanting to scream

when she tells me the story
it begins with everything is okay

and ends in a whisper and a smile
and her hand rubbing her leg

trying to bring it back to life

when we go
outside she holds

my arm to steady
herself in my life

her small hands
never leave my mind

and year after
year i watch her

in my memory
watch her knitting

on the couch
as i watch

twilight zone
by her alone

the way when she
rests them on her knees

when she pauses
and looks across

the living room
at me her son

but there is
another thing

that i can't leave
behind like grief

her voice just on
the other side of

the door my mother
telling my brother

how she is counting
the days until

i am gone far
away from her

house because she
can't handle me

anymore inside
those walls wide

enough to hold
a family lost

in a foreign and
fucked up land

he's crazy she said
your brother is crazy

i wasn't even
seventeen and

she'd told me so
often about god

and eternity
but never

about how one moment
with words spoken

would leave me
shattered shattering

each year older
my mind splitting farther

away from my body
that shakes alone

my heart bright
shards in the light

of the day as i try
to catch me

before even the grief
fades away

little tokyo

i visit them
in little tokyo
where they loved walking
around the block
by the ramen shops
and the bars
before the plague came

and we sit
at the table they've shoved
into the corner
by the kitchen
a giant rice cooker taking up
a third of the surface

and mom and i
watch my father die
between spoonfuls
of brown rice
and soup

i hold my breath
when she reaches for my arm
until neither of us
speak

one day
when i am important
during an interview
on television
they will ask me what it is
that i remember
about my life

and i will pause
to look at a light
glowing yellow
by the door
on the ceiling
before i answer

and the voice
that i hear
will catch me by surprise
as i tell them how
she reached for me
as my father was dying
and placed her hand
on my arm
to keep all of us
from falling

under my steps

the world
mother's hands

the war hidden
silence

under my steps
blood

a mid sentence pause
your bad morning

under my steps
talking

a wrist healing
the wind

under my steps
sharks

memories untrusted
the fires

under my steps
branches

me a boy
just that

sky song

there's always
a clear sky
when i remember

the night
when i die
by a tree

it is inevitable
like terror
and the house

is too far
for my mother
to see

that i held
my fists
tight

and still
lost
my heart

called the rain

she stepped outside
through the glass sliding
door with steps unsteady

it was spring already
before we could get our bearings
before we were done preparing

for the end of a hard winter
into the back porch where
the plants stolen in fragments

from hancock park pavement
when we could walk together
through breeze and gentler weather

while i waited by the grass
she'd lean into the plants lush
and green and thriving in the sun

just a little, she'd say, hush
they have plenty enough
and i would nod and shudder

at the wonder of this life
fading constantly into another
another realm then another

where her balance has never left her
her hands full of her score of the day
held together in front of her like a prayer

in the back porch she stood

and faced all that she had grown
all she had raised

lifted her arms lifting the pain
of this ending and called the rain
it was spring already

before we were were ready
before we could get our bearings
before we were done preparing

for the apocalypse
or the sound of a family
growing smaller

the last one

with each poem
i wrote
there was this wish
in my heart
like a child
a wish
a belief
that i was
getting closer
to discovering
myself
but like
all art
great and less than
it was all
illusion
no different
from my mother's
faith

it has been
almost 40 years
since i wrote
my first one
in high school
after a boy
with pretty hair
found me
alone
in the hallway
at uní high

i gripped tight

my inconceivable life
broken down
into the shapes
of stanzas
and pulled
myself out
into the sun
believing
now
god would
see me
and say

what
a great line
my son

you can
return home
my son

you can
return home

questions

if this is a song
i have to ask you questions

but you sat quietly
while dad yelled

because he was too tired
and i wasn't man enough

for his liking
you sat so quiet

and each time
i couldn't understand

why you'd abandon me
even as you could see

that i was disappearing

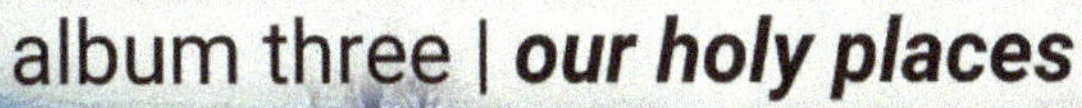

album three | our holy places

movement | the house | our holy places | a dream a scene a marriage
palisades | los ángeles, 2023 | pittsburgh, 2024 | new york, 2002
barcelona, 2006 | what i remembered of a future | santa clarita, 2024 | flight

album three

our holy places

inspired by

Dev Never • Reneé Rapp
Gracie Abrams • Taylor Swift
phoebe bridgers

movement

the mornings
waking up

on the sidewalk
of san pedro

in a car parked
in beverly hills

on a floor
next to strangers

and condom
wrappers

no longer sure
whether i was

trying to
figure out my life

or punish myself
into oblivion

when i was
a teen in los angeles

my father said
moving will lead

to constant moving
and it felt

like a warning
but now i see

it was a confession
for the curse

he'd brought
into my life

i'm in pittsburgh
on a tuesday night

writing and he is
in LA dying

and between us
there is a fire

that knows my name
swaying

like forgiveness
like forgetting

the house

i stood
at the dresser
trying to find
mother in the mirror
at the door
to the kitchen
bargaining
with death

but i didn't live there
in the house
of my childhood
with walls
built by ghosts
did i?

i stood
in the frozen yard
waiting for your hand
to touch me
in the back alley
crying and lost
in the dark corner
piss trickling
down my thigh

but did i ever
live in the house
in seoul
where memories
are stories made up
for the found

i stood
with my hand held
by a mother
who wasn't mother
crying for the mother
who was

in a room
that only exists
when i can't
breathe

i am sure
you imagine
those moments
are rare

but why
do you think
i have kept quiet
for so long

i stood
inside walls
that never heard
my name before
that couldn't echo
my grieving

but did i ever
live in the house
of a childhood
of a movie
that won't stop
dissolving

until all
that is left
to protect
my heart from
the cyclone
is my skin

our holy places

the bridges
and the rooftops
subway stations

so many
of our stories are
below us

in the rain
we held a chair
above our heads

until the seasons
rotated out
and the sun

melted us
into each other's
bones

so many
of our stories are
inside us

somewhere
between couscous
and belgian beer

we stopped
to kiss and tell
ourselves

that our lives

was our life
and that life

was a movie
where we kiss
on the sidewalk

in a new york
night and i thought
for once

so many
of our stories are
of us for us

and in one
just maybe
i could be

someone else
a name to be
remembered

as something
more than
a monster

a dream a scene a marriage

there was a dream
a scene
a marriage in a forest
somewhere so green
and lush

invisible
moving through
the crowd
in between
bodies
dressed so beautiful

i watched
judy walking
up the center
between the rows
of white chairs
in her wedding dress

the groom
i recognized him
someone famous
maybe a friend
i don't know anymore

after i opened my eyes
stared at the fan
spinning on the ceiling—
may weather has arrived
here in pittsburgh—
details started
to fade away

there was
a dream
a scene
where she found
happiness
possibility
for children
and i was a ghost
uninvited

a marriage
without
my madness and anger
without
having to keep me alive
pull my body
off the ledge
and back into
our bedroom

a dream

a scene

a marriage

a dream

palisades

stolen
like roses
from

a stranger's
garden
in the palisades

to pretend
i have something
to offer

at midnight
standing at
her door

she said
that it was
because

i was a coward
that would run
away

from
our baby
so this

was
what she
must do

and i

believed her
because

i didn't
know who
i am

who i was
meant to
become

what was i
supposed
to know

about the future
when my life
began

with a ghost
and
a nightmare

one day
some years
later

i stood
on a balcony in
downtown LA

celebrating
with childhood
friends

thinking
i was going
to be

a father
for real
this time

unaware
that what
would come

was all of this
unbearable
silence

los ángeles, 2023

i'm coming back to LA
across the storm of the century
through the jet black nights of utah
and the dragons hiding among the ruins

i'm coming to one of so many places
that i tried desperately to hold on to
the dust and the violence and the accents
that made the shape of home

but what will i do

if you no longer recognize me
if you no longer want me
if you no longer want to make
the sound of my name

where will i go

if i can't stop trembling
if i can't stop fracturing
if i can't wear the sound of your voice
to survive the war

i'm coming home
i'm coming home
i'm coming to the only place i've called home

but what will i do
but where will i go

if i can no longer run
through the

dark violent

gorgeous
hallways of your life

pittsburgh, 2024

cheap spanish wine
and the same song
about love and loss on loop

all the lights are off
and judy's long gone to bed
i've been trying to fight

off the train of panic
attacks coming at me
for the past 4 hours.

how do you grieve
something you don't know
you've lost? this morning

barbara told me
how she could feel the wave
of sadness coming from me

and i wanted her
to tell me that something
about my life makes sense

even if i am having flashbacks
of the moment before my own death
that i keep having memories

of places i have never been
that i don't think my family
is my real family

trying to stay awake

it's another night where
i am scared to sleep

it's a monday night
i am drinking
the waves

are still coming
and i think
i'm drowning

tell me

how do i learn to grieve my
life when i am still here

how will i learn to love it
when i am gone

new york, 2002

while sipping a glass
of cold barley tea

i was struck with a memory
of new york, 2002

it was of the night i died
falling from the rooftop

in downtown on broadway
the alley where i landed was quiet

it's a simple scene maybe not
simple but quite unexceptional

it goes like this:

>   i fall in the space between buildings
>   and i am looking through the darkness
>
>   at the bit of the night sky
>   i can see beyond the alley's darkness

it feels like i've remembered this before
the details of the night are familiar

it was never a scene from a movie
i'd watched crossfaded on tubi

but how could you blame me for not
realizing i was recalling my death

for being unable to consider

that this life that i remember having lived

the happiness the pain
the families breaking and building

the hands that i have held briefly
let slip out of my grasp

all the nights in dark rooms
wanting to know who i am

this life that i am learning to love
started only after mine was lost

barcelona, 2006

each morning
before she'd wake
i put on my clothes

and walk to
the argentinian bakery
for croissants

and a little extra
sweet treat for
my walk back

we were in barcelona
renting an apartment
for two months because

i wanted to die
and that was the only way
judy could keep me

from jumping out of
our 6th floor window
in downtown LA

there were the beaches
the black virgin in montserrat
the bocadillos at the square

wine and fucking
through paris
and florence

and with no money

left in our bank
or our credit cards

we took a photo
of her last pill
thinking of a future

that might be for us

there was another picture
we went up a mountain
and we stopped to rest

and i lay down
stared at the sky
how blue it seemed

i pointed my camera
and snapped a photo
and months after

we'd returned home
to los angeles
i looked at that picture

it was just a blue rectangle
and i couldn't remember
the rest of the day

then in a moment
desperate to hold on
to hope

i lost everything

what i remembered of a future

i told this story of the ghost
she was sitting on the stairs

it was our secret
mine and my father's

he'd tell this story and when he got to the part
where only he and i could see the ghost

he looked at me with
what i imagined was pride

it was soon after that
the nightmare came

of an empty classroom
and a woman i mistook for mother

or was it before
it was so long ago

in a place i am told i was born
it only matters that it never went away

what do you do with a life
that begins with terror

when the only thing that
you can hold on to is the fleeting

when i got older
the details fell away

the house got darker and emptier
even my father isn't there anymore

i've been off my medication
and there's been the hallucinations

but i started thinking
the dead i saw as a child was the ghost

of the daughter i would lose decades later
crazy right?

like i was gathering
all the possibilities of this

piling up all the connections
and raw materials

to convince myself this was true
me

an architect
trying to build myself

out of one house into another
where the air is easier to breathe

look
i spend the nights alone

drunk high
returning over and over

to the house in korea
that still stands in my mind

standing at the steps
until she returns

watching her lips move
trying to read the words

my child was saying to me
in this haunting

santa clarita, 2024

i had
the most
joyous time
tonight
in a theatre

while orbital
played waiting
became dancing
and
dancing
became
more
than i can say

i sat next to
the best human
in the world
and
remembered
all the
4 and 5 o'clock
mornings

holly golightly
sunrises
and
leaving
parties
until
i could arrive
at a life
i could cherish

growing up
in foreign lands
voiceless
and violent
i never thought
a man
in fucking
rollerblades
would break
my heart

there was a scene:

two people
swaying
like jellyfish
around and with
each other
back and forth
from and to
each corner
of the stage

and it was
gentle
the water
the ocean
in santa monica
and my father's voice
lifting my name
into the sky
until
i was an echo

and
the bodies
as i held on
to my seat
afraid of losing
myself
again
the bodies
kept moving
into and away
endlessly
living

flight

the temperature
won't go down at all

i have taken enough drugs
to imagine a less confusing life

it involves a lot of forgetting
but that part started long ago

we can't leave home without damage
your absence alters the landscape

there's a man next to me
who toasts with an empty cup

what can he possibly know
about my visions of burning castles

of hecate
and her wolves

what could he really know
about the storms trapped in my knees

voices are smoke on the verge of flight
i can almost taste your name in it

could i convince you to pause your travel
and rest on the shiver of my forearm

because i am high and i am tree and i am
wondering if there's a point in my breaking

where the dying
sounds like living

album four
exile

something counterfeit • clean me
never not mine • ice song
back where i started • the test
dream song • exile song
medicine • i have to believe that it is
late to hold • robin • the roof
let the world break your heart
strange light• por los siglos de los siglos

album four

exile

inspired by

**Finneas • Julien Baker
Reneé Rapp • boygenius
Taylor Swift**

something counterfeit

how do i say
good riddance
goodbye
to a lie
that i had to create
to survive

this memory is something
counterfeit i carried in my hands
to shield it from the bombs

all those days
and nights
in an empty house
in a land i was dropped on
and told to
learn the word
for home

languages
were something to wear
an ill fitting mess
that people mistook
for my skin

oh you have seen
the world, they say
you are lucky

you are lucky, they say
so lucky

there was always the sun

but also the winter
and my treasure carried across
so many borders
has turned to dust
that i can't keep from
flying away

how do i say
good riddance
goodbye
to a lie
that i had to create
to survive

in the sun
in the cold winter sun
my body
caught fire

and i thought
i heard him say
your bright future
is in my hands
shielded from the bombs

and you
will be the tree
that i plant in a place
you don't belong

nameless

to save the world
and whither alone

clean me

disappointments
will come in
shapes never seen

i am
on the couch
trying to see
in and through
the dark

the smell of
day old fish
lingers
in the hallway
like imagined
footsteps
even after the trash
has been taken out

my skin
lies about
my sins
like french music
in your mother's
history of wanting

i'm the echo
of your cup
hitting
the counter
when you
finished your
coffee

and left

never not mine

even as you're traveling
between stars between
galaxies for years now
you were never not mine

when i walk at night
i look up at the sky
it makes me feel like my
heart is floating away

more than once
i saw movement
for a moment and i thought
you were moving heaven

how do i call for you
beg you to return
when i no longer
know your name

what if goes only
one way too often
who would i have in a world
where i hold you?

but if i'm to be honest
i would have found a way
to fail you

everything and everyone
i have touched
has been bruised

you were never not mine
but your life was there for you
and only you to shape into
architecture to hold your heart

i am looking for movement
when you are moving heaven

what have you named yourself
tell me how to call you
home

ice song

this is ice, i say to her

but we are just walking out
of a bar around the corner

it's 4pm and summer has gone

and what i mean is

my fingers are curling
tight around cold air

listening to the screaming
inside me

what do you call this, i ask her

when i mean
how do i know
what to wish for her
when everything i want
turns muddy

how do i choose
between living
and a new thing

she says
this is sleet

but she means
hold out your arm
so i can hold on

to your broken elbow
as we walk

but she means
don't let me down
anymore

but she means
why couldn't we
have a child

this is ice, i say

and i mean
to tell her
that i am frozen
somewhere in a past
my body won't let me
send for

hold on
to my bent bones
because

i am

i am

slipping
away

back where i started

in the sun
by the window
with a black coffee

i put on my glasses
to read the news
and listen to the birds

or was it just
the one that comes back
over and over

right now
i saw the cloud move
and saw that it was too late

outside the window
in the sun where
all the birds have gone

right now
when i can't feel the sun
on my skin

and inside me
the nightmare is coming
i can feel its breath

the one
that comes back
over and over

the test

i never told my father
each morning when he left the house
felt like the test had begun
from some secret headquarters
where he'd watch me trying
to get through the obstacles he'd set

and I knew, and I knew
before any bell ringing
the start of the first class
he'd already seen me fall

i never told him
that i didn›t understand why
he never drove me to school
didn›t care that I counted
my steps each block I walked
so I wouldn›t get lost

in this secret exam, I questioned
why he never drove me home
leaving me to count my steps alone

but I knew, oh, I knew
before any judgement
could reach me that
he'd already seen me fall

his silence spoke
as he returned home (each night)
telling the story of my failure

I never told him

that every step was a plea
for him to see me dying

but one thing
i don't know still is

how could he be
disappointed
when nothing
was that thing
he expected

dream song

i saw myself in a dream
writing a poem

it was on a plane
the person next to me
eating a bag of mixed nuts

a flight attendant
walked past waiting
for a question

i saw myself in a dream
writing a poem

it was on my phone
as i always do now
muscle memory of that time
i didn't have a home

outside the window
the clouds moved
into the past of me

i saw myself in the dream
i was writing

and the poet
on the plane
turned to the dreamer

told him to wake up
and jot down the poem
as they were taught

and he cried
whispering

      i don't want to wake
      i don't want to wake

      i only want to remember
      this feeling of creating
      a miracle

exile song

i traced the map of home
on your back with my finger
as you slept turned away
from me. but when i returned
from my exile of fear
you'd shed your skin
to be born into the life
that was meant
for you and it was
too late too long
past too full of regret
to find the road curling into
the sky

alone
captive
learning

that living had always been
lonelier than god standing
in a land on fire feet bare
too busy with judgment
to hear my question about
the missing of my life

i traced my way
i raced my way
i chased your

forgiveness around
the sharp turn of your
hip away from me when i
reached for the barcelona sun

on the creases of
your skin in
slumber

the exile having been too long
to recreate the shape of hope
we made with our touch

in a burning room on a coast
far away from the first place i'd ever
wanted to call home

i've come back

but the road took almost
everything from me

the road

it took
almost
all of me

medicine

they mistook me
for a seed
and took me
across the ocean

i created a story
to tell myself
to sleep

in the story
there is a future
where i become
a tree

it's hard to unravel
the plot lines that
i drew on the board
just so i could rest

they mistook me
for a river in the night
with fish in it
waiting to die

drunken men
and their quiet wives
lost in their own
possibilities

i tell myself
that i will never forget
the night at their
dinner table

when they told me
everything was a lie
and my mind broke
like the rest of me

they mistook me
for medicine
for leaves that grow
and fall

and placed me
in the sun
proud of what
they had done

they didn't see
i was burning
until i had to leave
my body behind

locked and empty
the seasons
tearing its walls apart
my heart exposed

they mistook me
for their own destiny
for the reply to
their prayers

and stayed too busy
speaking to god
to ask me if i miss
my own child

the one that left us
in confusion
on a downtown morning
that promised sun

at nights after
i sit in the dark
silent to listen for
her voice

calling to me
from the home
that she has found
calling to me

they mistook me
for their survival
and didn't notice
i was terrified

of all the things
that i have seen
that i have failed
in becoming

i have now moved
over thirty times
the thing is i lost
me long time ago

all the things
i was supposed to be
tree medicine
son father

we mistook ourselves
for a family
each other
for answers from god

i have to believe that it is

when the hurricane called for me
my hand closed until there was
a shape i could feel in my palm
like love or the way my knees bled
while praying on a dirt field in asunción.

i have to believe that this is how
it was meant to end, this book of
my family—far from home, quiet
as the world burns around us. i have
to believe that this is what my father

wanted, needed, no different than
what i've sought all my life:
to run to disappear to change
a predetermined outcome so the
nightmares couldn't find us anymore.

back to my closed fist—

i will call this shape i hold
a bird and i am dying because
i'm too scared of suffocating it
and too terrified of letting it fly away.

late to hold

the storm was unexpected
the forecasts had been wrong
and i stayed on the road
turned around and lost for too long

the pavement beneath my feet
kept changing its skin
from rocks to grass to sand to black
asphalt, tar, melting

the way home is never
the way you left in reverse
that path wipes away behind you
a parlour trick at your circus

the way home is never
toward the light contained
so bright that even
death looks like day

and by the time i entered
the house of my childhood
it was dark and the steps
were empty like the rooms

who do i call for
when i can't remember calling
for anyone

who do i look for
when nobody accompanies me
through my nightmares

then i found you in mother's secret room
i remember now—exactly where i left you

forgive me for forgetting
how small you were and how scared
standing at her vanity holding her bra
to your butt cheeks because

what was i supposed
to know about bodies hidden
or a future or a journey
that i would have no say in

i didn't remember there
was never anyone here
how could i forget such a detail
and be so late to hold you

but now that i am here
now that i have returned
which one of us sparkles away
which one of us gets to let go

this storm was unexpected
the forecasts were wrong
and i was lost on the road
in motion for too long

this road
to forgiveness
this road
with the storm

i never thought
any of it would
finally end

robin

i felt so close to death
to an afterlife i lacked
the faith to enter

those 3am drives home
keeping my eyes closed
on sunset blvd turns

while on the run
from another house
another bed another—

i made her my lighthouse
and sailed toward her
from the dark sea

she saw me only drowning
couldn't hear me scream
how i wanted the shore

i placed my lips
on her shoulder
and in her house i saw

the ghost
she carries

and in the dark
i left her quietly

and halfway down
her driveway i'd forgotten
how to return

another house
another bed
another 3am escape

our bodies since
have broken
healed to break again

i don't close my eyes
too often anymore
well at least not in a few weeks

and every so often
when i see a light far away
i remember

how for a short time
the darkness in front of me
became smaller

the roof

we stood
opposite each other
joking about
how much
she had bled

and pointed
at the red dots
on the sheets
and the bigger
stain on the pillow
that she held between
her knees

in my mind
i am still
sitting on the couch
by the window
turned to her
because
she was lit
from within

and she said

    the world is coming
    to a fast end
    and i want
    to get back
    to myself

it's a funny thing
that happens

inside me
in moments
of small and
big explosions
here and far
away

i thought in the end
there would be a memory
i hang on to

we were on
her roof in brooklyn in
each other's arms in
new york's night sky

and she was
waiting for me
to stay
she was waiting
for me to
be ready

and i felt
all of it
past present
future
at the same time

and i wanted
nothing more
than to stay

and i wanted
nothing more

than to be

someone who
could get ready

and i wanted
nothing more
than to know

the secret to holding
the night so tight
that it
would never
leave me

let the world break your heart

i stopped believing
there was honesty
in my writing
the same way
i stopped waiting
for them to tell
me the truth of me

when i was a child i dreamt
of a crowd an audience
that never came
only to learn somewhere
between panic attacks
that i was only always
trying to get myself to hear me

here i am now shuffling
through all my poems
trying to wrap myself in
a love that i thought was
meant for someone else

whispering

    you did it
    you survived
    you let the world
    break your heart
    again and again

these words
this writing is evidence
that i have lived

some proof
that i wanted
to find a way
to love myself
and failed so many times each day

i want to tell this body

        i forgive you for not knowing
        how to accept yourself

i wish i'd been taught that mercy
was mine to gift myself in an emergency

your inability to hear my voice
gave me the freedom to speak
even though when i was alone
i hoped you'd call me beloved

oh my fucking god
i can't stop hopping around
all over the place
in this fucking poem

but i'm tired and scared
and broken or breaking
or whatever you want to say i am
because i spent another night
chasing my body around the apartment
"depersonalized"—a new word
i learned this week from someone
who just wants me to live

each time that
i think maybe

i can love myself—
but don't you know
that i am terrified
that it's too late
that it's too late
to change my life
and i'll have
to lose myself
again

so i want to ask you
(by you i mean mom. or dad. god.)
the memories that you gifted me
through stories and prayers
who did they belong to
before they became mine
because i keep getting lost
while trying to find
my place of birth

i've been counting my poems
the way i count the days
something in the way
the air touches my body
colder than i expected
making me feel this one
is the last one

so just in case it is
i think maybe
i found a thought
worthwhile
for me anyway
in each thing in my life
that ends

the poem
the day:

that forgiveness is a destination
a hard fought lesson

about…
something.
something that matters, ok?

because i don't know
what the sun
will say to my skin
tomorrow
when it reaches out
its hand
and wraps its fingers
around
my body
that won't stop
falling apart.

strange light

she touches
the strange light
of my body
and takes flight

back into
the raging battles
inside her own
house rattling

on this earth
in mid-implosion
and in this morning
of confusion we talk

over black coffee
and granola
about choosing
death in canada

because fighting
leaves only blood
without flowers
blooming god

she is the light
she has always been

even when her body
shattered slowly then fast
like a world that craters

beneath our feet

from the weight of
our collective fear while trying
to create a place

where we can love each
other fully and this thing
of death can't bother us

she touched me
this strange light
and counted my breaths
with me until night
came.

por los siglos de los siglos

i hope

in one of
all the
lifetimes

to come

i'll stop
disappointing
you.

SKY SONGS is done. it's broken up into four albums:
"somewhere murmur," "ugly," "our holy places" & "exile."
it's messy and repetitive and maybe the worst of my 5
books. but i love it. it feels like the first book i've written
to me, for me to read. and that was worth the journey of
this book—which started in 2010, the first time i heard
taylor's "Fearless" and decided what i really wanted my
writing to be is just a direct line to my emotions and
confusions, my fears and my anxieties. the messy stuff.
— chi

*

Published by
Writ Large Press
a division of Writ Large Projects
writlargeprojects.com

ISBN: 979-8-88757-180-5

Photos of Flowers by
Melora Walters

Written & Designed by
Chiwan Choi

*

2024